Gods Plan to Succeed while Healing

Chapters

THE RUDE AWAKENING

I....Don't come for me

II....Love don't cost, your life do

II....The Humiliation

IIII....Breaking point to determination

V....Trust your gut with Gods Words

VI....Family First Till Death do us part

VII....Spiritual Healing

VIII....Power

THE RUDE WAKENING

How many women see themselves as survivors, a woman that heal from her abuser, attacker, haters, and humiliators.

I say "around of applause" once those stones been thrown your way it takes one hell of a woman to break through those scars and back on track like nothing never happened.

In this story that's exactly what Shanel is all about.

Her life activities as a survivor and a single mother of three.

CHAPTER I

DON'T COME FOR ME

"Hey Cutie Hey what's your name" as I hear a male voice going down the mall escalator, I looked back of course I didn't see anyone so I continued to go on with what I attended to do.

Seventeen years old working in a mall as a food prep was not the work I was going for after graduation, but I did it and did it well.

"Hey girl now I know you heard me calling you the first time why you didn't answer me, What's your name."

I looked and stared for a second I was like excuse me is that how you approach me.

So I walked back to my place of work as the male watched me walk, he mumbled something, I was not able to hear let alone to care.

"Girl what's wrong with these men they think they can come for me anyway and I suppose to be ok with it."

As I started to explain the situation to my friend Latrina that worked in the restaurant next door to me.

The more I talked to her it was like she wanted to say something but she held it in until I finished.

"Girl What!!! Why you starring at me like that" I stated.

That's Lamont girl a nobody that tried to talk to me and Terri but it didn't go anywhere.

The rolling of my eyes as I walked away off my break.

I'm so ready to go home is it 5'0clock yet as my mind wondering thinking about Lamont, and all the what if's.

Latrina and her friend (Terri) did they date him, have sex or just flirt my mind was all over the place.

I don't know, it's 5pm time to go home and guess who I see as I'm leaving going down the escalator stairs (LAMONT).

"if I speak again will you speak back this time" Hello Beautiful!!!! My response with a smirk HI!

Before he can say anything else I blurted out didn't you try to holla at my girl that work in the restaurant next to me (shoulder shrug) that's what I heard!!!

This way it will stop him from any other conversations.

"Dam Girl that's how you feel I wasn't trying to holla at nobody all I asked was your name" but that's ok as he turned away looking all handsome.

I just knew I was playing hard to get but he looked like one of those player type men.

Long Wave nouveau, brown skin, big eyes and sexy lips I was like SHANEL!!!!!!

"MY NAME IS SHANEL OK YOU HAVE IT" he turned, looked at me and said got it Shanel with a smile.

I smiled ear to ear going down the escalator like dang he's fine but I will continue to play hard to get until I can figure this man out, he might want to be friends I don't know, I will give him the benefit of the doubt if he approach me again.

"RING RING" RING RING it's 11pm who's calling me this late knowing I have to be at work, this better be important.

"HEEELLLOO" in my cute and sexy sleepy voice.

Hello hello how you doing this Lamont, "Lamont!!!! Lamont who?"Acting like I don't know.

Boy how you get my number I didn't give it to you, and you have the audacity to call me at 11 O'clock at night you must be feeling lucky.

Calm down Ma, you aggressive I got your number from Latrina since y'all talk about me so much.

I felt like I should call you but I see you mind.

Thinking to myself I know this tramp did not give my number to this man, and she told him we talk about him.

Now I see why I don't have female friends why she do that!!

"Boy don't nobody sit and talk about you!! Sorry you not that important."

His voice sound so good on this phone as I laid up and crossed my legs listening to him go on and on about how beautiful I am when he see me walking through the mall.

Thinking to myself like why is he always there.

Then it came out you know I work at Foot Action Shoe store.

Oh ok well I'm tired it's 2 o'clock and we talked all this time I have to be at work it's time I talk to you later.

Before I could say anything he told me I sounded tired so he will let me go to have a good night sleep and he will see me in the morning.

This guy keep coming for me, he just won't let go so let's see what he's on tomorrow when we see each other.

7am tired with a slight headache but I have to get to work "oh my goodness I can't wait to get a car I'm so tired of catching this bus".

Standing on the bus stop, cold with a big coat and earmuffs thinking and wishing I was picked up right about now!

" HEY SHANEL" this guy never miss a beat do he.

Hi! I will see you later on my lunch break as I proceeded to walk off the escalator toward the restaurant to open up.

"Tramp you sure do have a lot of nerves giving Lamont my phone number".

What type of friend are you besides one of the fake ones.

As we both were opening the restaurant doors to walk in apparently Latrina thought it was funny but I thought she was wrong.

"Girl get over yourself he asked about you I told him to call for himself if he's inquiring that much.

it's not like you didn't want him to have it".

She's one of those messy friends that don't care about nothing if it's not about her, but yes I'm ok with him having my number.

It's time I get to know more about him.

Every man have a story to tell about there life when talking to a woman, they want you to know the good, bad and what they want.

But they never talk about there ugly side and that switch that turns off and on.

"Can I have the Steak combo 1 with extra steak, you and a Mountain Dew" How are you today miss lady didn't see you walk pass, what time you off maybe we can hang out later after work I will pick you up.

Starting to ring up Lamonts order I was like here we go this guy really don't stop do he.

Something he want so let me entertain it to see where it goes.

"Tonight will be great I will be ready around 7pm, I will call you with my address".

Lamont grabbed his order as he started to walk away I hear a soft voice in the air "Hi Lamont", Latrina walking by.

She had to make it known that she know him as well. "Lamont what's on your agenda I want to see you".

I'm looking like this thirsty heifer now she wants attention when it's not on her anymore.

When a man that approaches a woman that's blown off and the attention is no longer there a woman will find a way to get it back.

"Hey Latrina thanks but I'm good!!!

I have plans maybe next time", walking away smiling at me which made me melt.
I'm so ready what should I wear?

This man like 21 years old and I'm only 17 this should be interesting fresh out of high school talking to a man older then me, what will my dad say I already know my mom but dad he's not going to take it well.

Time went fast must of known that I have date so it's 6:45pm already called with my address so I'm ready.

Hair check, outfit check I'm all natural so I will see what Lamont have to say when he see me, good thing dad not here he's still working so this will be a good night.

"SHANEL!!! What are you doing you don't hear the doorbell ringing" as my mother yelling from the kitchen.

So I put on my lipgloss as I opened the door all I see is that wave nouveau and his smile, I heard him say you ready baby.

Unbelievable he open the passenger door ok a gentleman let's see what else he have up his sleeve.

Where is he taking me, we riding music loud and I'm thinking should we have conversations of just sit and listen to the music.

"WHERE WE GOING?" Looking at him in suspense this ride seem so long from North Ave to Wauwatosa in silence.

He looked at me with the reply Ponderosa baby, have you eaten there before.

NO!!! By the name it sounds nice.

So he have a point for opening my door but a strike for this long silent ride and loud music.

Some women can deal with all the loud music most can't but I most definitely survived it I'm on a date let's enjoy he seem like a cool dude to think we have all night to make conversation he probably was thinking of what to say and how to say it (Shrug shoulders).

Shrimp, Macaroni, Fish, Spaghetti with the sweet cornbread. "Baby do you eat Shrimp taste this and I will be back".

He proceeds to get up and go to the rest room as I dip the shrimp in the sauce and swallow the entire thing now I'm gagging.

Something not right I thought I was suppose to break off the tail, now I'm feeling sick and embarrassed.

I can't believe I swallowed a whole shrimp what do I do he's walking back to the table and all I can do is look at him until he say something.

You good what's wrong did you taste it?

Yes!!

I swallowed the entire thing, I'm guessing I had to much wine earlier I wasn't able to catch the tail before it went down!

We laughed continued conversation until it was time to leave, I have to say the night went well all smiles with ending the night with a passionate hug.

The following day off work in my room watching television my phone rings guess who? Terri (Latrina's best friend) what do she possibly want.

"Hey girl so I heard you and Lamont was messing around, you know he tried to take me out too."

I want to hang up this phone, why do females like to be so messy.

I'm like ok and you telling me this why it's a free world he tried, it didn't happen let's carry on what's next.

"Oh ok that's good you didn't want him I see but any who he's on the way over here now, matter of fact girl I hear my door bell, I will see you tomorrow when I get back to work peace" (heifer). Hanging up my phone not caring if she was still on it or not.

Women like Latrina and Terri are the messy type of ladies that talk about you one day, but in your face trying to hang out the next.

They suck in all the information to use it against you.

Door bell ringing my mom opens the door I thought it was Lamont surprise it's my high school friend/ex Domo he's out of jail.

What a distraction why he didn't call me popping up at my house like this, unbelievable and Lamont's on the way.

"Hello Ms. Houston Shanel home?" Thought I would stop by just made it home a couple days ago and wanted to see her.

"You looking nice Domo always good to see you sweetie Shanel Domo at the door."

Pacing back and forth what should I do, should I tell him I'm dating and want nothing to do with him or just have mom tell him to come back.

So I decided to face him telling him it was over and my reason why nothing I expected or wanted to happen but I feel it's the right decision.

"Hey Dominique why you didn't call me so I would of known you were coming.

Thinking to myself I needed to know to prepare myself in case Lamont show up. You know better then popping up over my house like this.

"Well dam baby why you acting jumpy can I have a hug a kiss or something acting like you see a ghost."

I miss you too, looking trying to make sure I don't see a golden brown Chevy pull up.

"Domo you have to leave since you been locked up I been dating another man that I want to be with."

Dealing with you in and out of jail is too much for me.

I need a stable relationship without all the extra that comes behind it, the fire that was coming from Domo eyes as he was staring at me.

Looking like why am I doing this to him right now I tried to hug him he pushed me away like a horrible smell.

My intentions was not to hurt you I just want better and I know my dad will not want us together with everything your doing and how you living, It will not work I'm sorry.

Loud music getting closer and closer to my house as I see that golden brown Chevy.

"Ok Dom you have to leave I already know how you are and how you act can you go please," as I hugged and pushed him off my porch to walk away with pain in his eyes.

We never discussed a relationship when he got out, but he wanted it knowing we were better off as friends then partners. I will always love Domo as he love me.

You will never know if the grass greener until you test it to see for yourself.

CHAPTER II

LOVE DON'T COST YOUR LIFE DO

5pm on the East side with my sister hanging out talking and having drinks. I received a phone call from Domo with his passionate deep voice, "Good evening Shanel" I hope your better then those last couple of months after I left your moms house, I haven't heard from you I hope everything ok.

"Hey Dom I'm good sitting at sis house kicking it but yes I'm over all that, you made your point when you decided to show off your gun so I'm good," closing my cell phone as he decided to call back to back until I answered.

"Girl I know Lamont is not blowing you up like that so who keep calling you?" As my sister Milly asked looking all Buck-eyed with the rolling of her neck and the smacking of her tongue.

Nobody Girl Mind your business!!! Yelling from the living room table "Lamont suppose to be Down South with his family."

My sister so extra and nosy I heard her say suppose to be!! You don't know where your man at? A Text message coming through from Domo is he yelling at me?

"CAN I SEE YOU PLEASE IM SORRY, I MISS YOU ITS BEEN A LONG TIME SHANEL TO COME HOME AND SEE YOU WITH ANOTHER MAN THAT YOU SAY YOU WANT IN YOUR LIFE, KNOCKING ME OUT YOUR LIFE AFTER ALL WE BEEN THROUGH I LOVE YOU".

Reading Dom text, he knew how upset I was with him but I have to be fair giving him a chance to sit and talk.

2237 N. 2nd Street Apt 3 as I texted back I will give him a chance to speak his peace and leave.

I need a harder drink let me go to the liquor store before they close it's 8:40pm, especially with Dom coming he's feeling some type of way I don't have time to be shedding tears over spoiled milk my dad always said to me (slight grin).

"SIS I'LL BE BACK!!! Going to the store as I walked out closing the door.

Shanel!!! Shanel!!! Yep I know that voice deep and sexy as I turn around and see Domo.

"Hey Dom omw to the store, walk with me it's about to be a long night dealing with you" as we both laughed walking into the store.

I think I want something really hard to take my mind off everything what should I get with this orange juice, looking into the cooler (I already know Domo about to say something).

"Dam girl what you doing drinking Gin, you trying to get messed up or something." I knew that was coming knowing he's a smoker and I'm a drinker.

Boy what ever you smoke, I drink.

$21.90 said the cashier with a smile on his face. You smiling too hard sir, I must be his last customer for the night.

"I got this baby with yo fine ass, man I can't believe you picked this clown over me" as Domo paid for the drinks starting to walk out back to my sister's apartment building.

"TOOK YOU LONG ENOUGH" Yells Milly I see why!! Whats up Dominique I know you have a blunt.

Milly don't see nothing more then weed she don't drink but get high as a kite and Domo was ready to roll one.

"I got you sis" as he looking at me like I should be with him instead of Lamont.

Ring ring ring ring wow he would call now, leaving the kitchen to walk into Milly's room ring ring ring "HELLO!!!

"Hey baby!!" Why you calling so late" all I can see is that brown skin and sexy lips. "You must be sleep, I wanted to hear your voice.

Just finished hanging out with cuz reminiscing and shit!!" As he repeats the question, you sleep?

"No Lamont at Milly's house having drinks, playing cards and talking".

I couldn't finish my sentence before Domo walked in the room rubbing on my shoulders to my back.

"Alright then enjoy and call me in the morning," hanging up like he was upset.

Domo wanted attention so he decided to barge in on my conversation.

"Really why you do that I don't have time for your shenanigans Dom I thought you wanted to talk".

We have more then enough time right now to tell me what's on your mind.

Room of silence all I felt was big wet lips across mine as I wanted to pull back but I didn't, I continued to kiss him back knowing it would go to far!

"Boy what you doing as I snatched back!"

What I wanted to do months ago! I love you Shanel nothing I won't do for you, I want to make love to you.

I don't want you to go Shanel you suppose to be with me not that dude (Grabbing my hands rubbing them with his thumbs).

He's definitely about to make me emotional knowing I have to tell him what's really going on with me and why I'm not with Lamont right now.

"Domo I have Chlamydia!!!!

As tears fall from my brown eyes not knowing what he's thinking. "Chlamydia Shanel so that nasty ass dude spreading diseases and shit!!!"

I knew he wasn't right for you now I see why I had that gut feeling to kill his ass right then and there.

Dominique is that type of guy you don't want to play with, he's like a terminator kill with no hesitation nobody can calm him down besides myself or his mom.

I feel cold lips across my neck up to my lips with a very passionate kiss that lasted until my shirt was off and my nipples were cold.

The love, compassion, seduction and sensation was most definitely taking over which Domo didn't care about my situation.

"Dom you have to stop did you forget what I told you!!!" DOM STOP!!!! As it got hotter and hotter in the moment that he was inside of me.

OH MY GOD!!! Laying there as a tear fall from my eyes down my face.

"Baby we good whatever you go through I will too, the love I have for you mean more then anything I feel like if I can't have you nobody can. "Stop crying man you good."

Shit at this point I don't know what to think anymore I need to pray!

What's going on here, we went from conversation to sex.

"Dominique are you happy now this was not suppose to happen and I allowed it knowing I have."

SSSSSHHHHHHH BABY DIDN'T I TELL YOU DON'T WORRY ABOUT IT!

As Dom looked at me with this look in his eyes that I never seen before, he keep telling me not to worry but how can I not, I guess he thought I was lying either way he showed me it don't matter to him I'm all he wants and he will not stop until he gets me.

The quiet music and loud snoring everybody in the house sleep as I'm up pacing the floor in deep thought talking to myself.

"Shanel get it together girl he said you ok then you ok god got this all I need to do is pray and go to sleep."

Never allow your guards to go down especially to a man you barely know verse a man that you do. When he loves you he will never do anything to hurt or harm you.

The weekend finally over back to work and Lamont will be back the next day.

"Shanel come here!!! Milly told me Dominique was over there! Why that boy spending the night at your sisters house you know better then that."

As my mother opens the door to my bedroom with her act like a lady attitude.

Milly talk to much! "Ma, I know better he wanted to talk and we end up falling asleep."

"What the hell who getting flowers!!! I said who getting flowers" Dad yelling as he leaving out the front door for work and met the flower delivery guy walking up.

"Good morning Sir do Shanel live here," I think this beautiful flower bouquet is for her.

Smiling as he speaks to my dad.

My dad have the worst attitude, loving man but he's mean he don't play no games when it come down to his baby girl.

22 white roses the card reads:

Shanel you are the most beautiful woman I met in my life, these white roses mean exactly what you are and I will never take anything from your innocence.

Young love and eternal loyalty these roses symbolize a new beginning and everlasting love.

Always know that I love you and will forever be with you

Love Dom,

After I read the card that came with the roses I was totally stunned saying "wow Dominique Love don't cost but people lives do especially playing around with ones heart."

Mom standing by my door staring with a slight smile, Well your dad gone to work what time do you leave?"

Knowing she have more then that to say to me.

I'm leaving about 9:45am mom, by the way the flowers from Domo as I looked at her with the slant in my eyes.

I already knew where she was going with our conversation my mom is like the old lady on 227 that sit on the ledge at her apartment.

Love her to pieces but between my mom and Milly, mom's the most nosiest of the two.

9:45am let me get to work its the 1st of the month so my day will be busy and full of weirdos.

"Shanel your shift started at 9am why are you a hour and 20 minutes late!" As Sonya the petite long hair brunette blurts out, seeing me walk into the door.

"Sonya what are you talking about my start time says 10:45 you should know you made the schedule, replying back with my, I can't stand her attitude.

She's a new manager walking in here with her nose in the air not knowing anything besides who she wants to fire.

"Shanel since you want to be a smart ass how about you prep this morning until I need you on the floor!"

This lady have me all screwed up, I knew I was about to have a weird day but I expect it to come from the customers and not management.

So before I act out, lady I rather walk out this door and wait to receive my paycheck.

"Sonya you will not talk to me like that especially knowing I did nothing wrong so don't worry about me being on the floor or prepping because I QUIT!!"

Walking out slamming the door.

"What's wrong with you girl?" Latrina asked standing at the back of the restaurant with her cigarette in one hand and the other hand on her hip.

"Nothing that need to be explained just know I will no longer be working here." As I started walking down the street toward the bus stop. I don't care who you are I act accordingly, and talk to you the way you spoke to me.

"What's up Shanel you good girl?"

So I heard you know longer working at the mall, as Terri look at me walking in the grocery store on North. "Sucks to be you!" With her bright red lipstick and fully curled wig.

"NO TERRI IT SUCKS TO BE YOU WALKING OUT THE HOUSE LOOKING LIKE SOMEBODIES KID CLOWN,".

Thinking to to myself did she try to down me about working for $6.50 a hr let me go home I don't have time for this, pushing my cart to my dads car after grocery shopping for the house.

"Hey baby did you get everything?"

You know your daddy love his pig feet's and hog mols you didn't forget the vinegar did you SHANEL?

"Shanel what's wrong with you are listening to me," as mom staring into my face as is I was def.

"Yes mom I have everything, I was just thinking about the type of work field I want to be in now that I'm not working at the mall anymore".

I feel so humiliated with everything that's been going on I can't seem to get anything right, as I started walking to my room holding my head down in shame and sadness.

My new phone ring tone playing as I answer seeing that it's Lamont calling with nothing positive to say besides "WHATS ON YOUR AGENDA TODAY?"

"Hey Lamont what's up, as I answered the phone softly!!,"

What's up baby girl, why you sound like that like you sad? "What's on your Agenda I'm back in town I want to see you.

"Not today Lamont, I'm not in the mood I was about to shower and crawl into my bed my stomach feel funny and I'm irritated about how my day went".

I really didn't have much conversation for him my mind going every which way.

Thinking about my past weekend with Domo, this STD Lamont gave me and he's acting like everything ok.

My job, Terri and her Clownish ways, my stomach ache it's just so much!

As I started crawling into my bed with all these thoughts racing in my head thinking why me!!!

After telling Lamont I didn't want any company he repeats " Baby so I can't come over?"

I just looked at my phone and said "I will call you later because apparently you didn't listen to anything I said".

I should of known he wasn't the one for me then but something kept me close to him in his arms.

Hanging up my phone, I started looking for something more relaxed then what I had on after my shower.

RING Ring Ring "oh my goodness can I get in the shower", stomping across the floor to grab my phone whose calling me now, as I go to answer the call the ringing stopped, unknown number.

"If they want anything they will call back," as I walked back to the bathroom to take a long and relaxing bubble bath.

Hot water steamed water, Victors Secret seductive bath wash, aromatherapy sea-salt, candles and soft meditation music.

Looking for my Loofah and talking to myself "I just need to relax and think without any interruptions.

Getting into my bath tub as my feet cover up in bubbles feeling so good to my body as I lay down feeling the sea salt rub across my buttock, legs and back what a relaxing sensation.

The relaxation of a woman's body to purify her mind and soul!

SHANEL, "I know this child didn't fall asleep in the tub!" SHANEL!!!!

Hurry up and come out the bathroom, listening to my mom yell and knocking on the door.

I was too relax to answer or say anything, so I let her talk and knock until I was ready to come out.

Stepping out the tub with my wet body, bubbles going across my arm and legs as I stepped on our yellow flush bath rug grabbing a hold of my towel.

Nice bubble bath, meditation and concentration I can't feel any better then this walking out the bathroom with my towel wrapped around me as I walk into my room.

LADIES WHY PUT EACH OTHER DOWN MAKING ONE ANOTHER FEEL LESS THEN THE OTHER.

**ITS TIME WE LIFT EACH OTHER UP TAKING AWAY THE HATE/ENVY/BAD ATTITUDES, REPLACING IT WITH
LOVE/PROSPERITY/HAPPINESS and GRATITUDE.**

"I wonder if her ass mad at me, shit I never did nothing wrong to her, I know her ass not still tripping over that Chlamydia bull."

Lamont talking as he's best friend Corey passing the blunt.

"Chlamydia Bro!!!" Hell yea she's mad I'm mad for her dawg, what was you thinking".

I thought you said you liked that girl I say you bogus, smoke going into the air as Corey exhale.

A MAN THAT LOVES HIS WOMAN WILL NEVER HURT YOU.

HE WILL DO AS MUCH AS HE CAN IN HIS POWER TO PROTECT HER, KEEPING HER OUT OF HARMS WAY.

DAWG!!!! "Who side you on, how was I suppose to know I thought Terri was cool you know we been messing around for a while.

Her shit good but not as good as my girl. I have to make this up before it's too late, Lamont laughing and chuckling with Corey grabbing his phone to call Shanel.

ANSWER YOUR PHONE BABY!!! Ring ring ring

"IT'S SHANEL YOU MISSED ME OR I JUST DON'T WANT TO ANSWER LEAVE A MESSAGE I WILL HIT YOU BACK PEACE".

Dam did she send me to the voicemail we doing voicemails now.

Lamont looking at his phone like it will be something different so he called back and there was no answer.

NEVER GET A WOMAN SO FED UP, TO THE POINT SHE DON'T WANT TO BE BOTHERED WITH THE MAN SHE SUPPOSE TO LOVE.

"She playing games, I have to pop up on her ass.

I told her I was sorry what she want me to do!"

"What time is it Bro?" it's like 7:45pm I know she's not sleep this early.

I should of known something was wrong when she didn't want to see me.

Corey looking at Lamont, Lamont looking back at Corey I'm going to her house she got me fucked up!!!

It feels like she have another man over there, as Lamont talking feeling a little insecure.

"Let her breathe bro, you cheated on her and slept with somebody without protection, how you expect her to feel".

Listening to Corey as he replies back with his deep tone.

"Let her be for now call her tomorrow."

Lamont don't like to wait he need to know if Shanel with another man.

He started pacing the floor, rolling blunts, after blunts until he was so high he went to sleep on the couch.

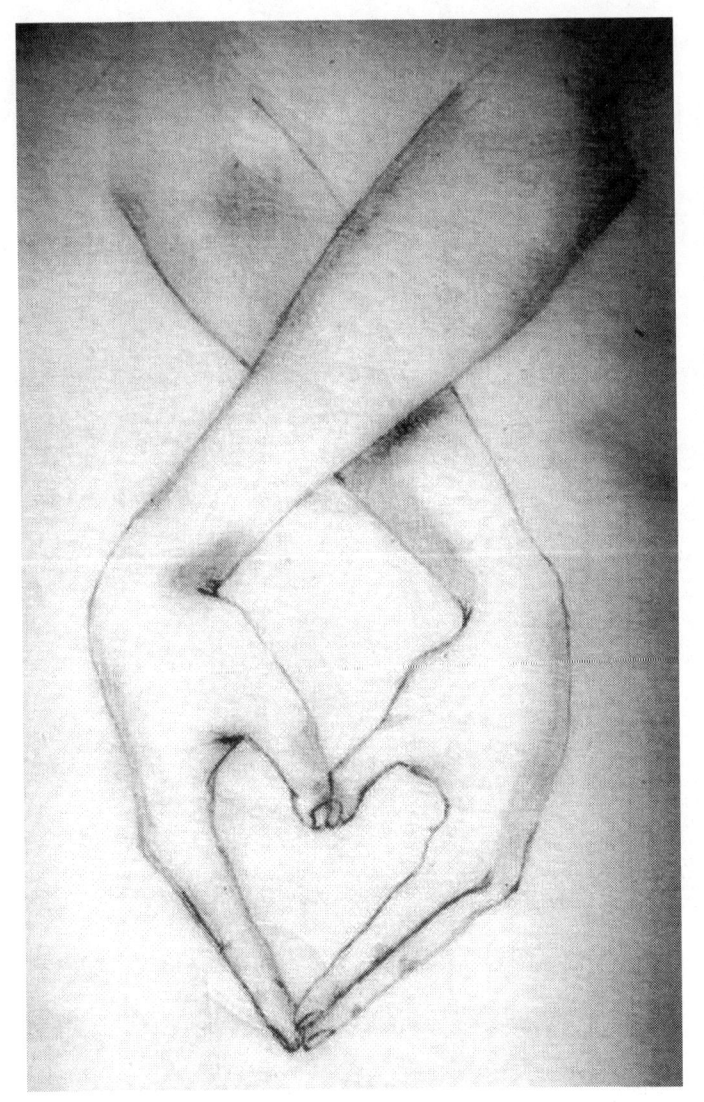

WHY CHEAT ON THE ONE YOU LOVE WITH SOMEONE YOU CARE NOTHING ABOUT, NEVER MAKE HER FEEL LESS THEN SHE SUPPOSE TOO.

CHAPTER III

THE HUMILIATION

May 10, 1998 10 o' Clock in the morning, how time flies!

I graduated from high school, worked in a mall where I met many of friends and associates well as the man I love.

As time went by he started to show me the worst of him.

I started to ignore him and his calls so I could figure out what I wanted to do.

Do I love him to leave or enough to stay, Staring at the wall in my bedroom before I leave for work.

SHANEL!!!!! "Come here", yelled my father as he sits on the couch, legs crossed arm on the arm rest looking at me with his Slanted eyes.

"What's up dad, you good"?

Yea girl, I wanted to talk to you just to see how my baby girl been doing since you haven't been with that boy!

I know he been doing wrong by you.

God will handle it, if it's meant to be then let it if not let it go.

You my baby and I can't see no man hurting you.

I taught you better then that! To love him not hard but the same, a man will love his woman/wife more because he plan to give her the world without hurting her.

I love you baby always remember gods plan to love, give and live not to be humiliated.

As I started walking away from my dad "I love you more daddy thank you".

It's time I get ready and leave for work I have a new job at this bagel place let's see how this all goes.

I feel like it's the first day of school.

Walking out the house "BYE MOM BYE DAD". Sounding like a kid on the way to catch the bus!

This again I need money, I need a car, I need my own house and a better paying job or career.

All my friends making money and have there own cars, lord when will my time come.

Thirty-five minutes to get to work It's my first day, so let's see what's all in store for the day.

As I was taking my jacket off to put on my apron.

"WELL GOOD MORNING YOUNG LADY"! Hearing a man voice with a Squeak to it.

"You must be Shanel, I heard about you from your interview, management loves you girl that's what I'm talking about you haven't even started yet and your talked about"!

Well my name is Terrance I'm one of the day shift workers always my pleasure to meet a pretty lady.

Looking at me with a smile and a slight laugh.

"Hello Terrance, nice to meet you yes I'm Shanel Thank you!"

Starting my shift watching Terrance as he greet the customers, giving great customer service and a friendly attitude as he's making there bagel sandwiches.

This is way different then the first job in the mall. It's way more smaller and quiet but it's ok.

I noticed many Jewish couples that came in today they love how Terrance make there bagels with his little twist of the different meats and cream cheese.

"It's 4:45 Shanel I can handle the rest you did good on your first busy day".

Listening to Terrance as he pop his lips and snapped his fingers.

Terrance so handsome but so feminine everything's perfect on him.

Carmel smooth skin, plucked eyebrows, white teeth, clean shave and cut with his tucked shirt into his pants.

"YESSS HONEY YES YOU BETTER WALK", all I heard after punching out and walking out the door.

Terrance about to be a hand full with fun written on it! He made me feel extremely comfortable today.

Looking at my cellphone, I see seven missed calls and three text messages.

"Shanel I told you I was sorry baby what more do you want from me! Take me back you will see a change I need you".

Lamont don't understand I'm not ready for him to be in my life, he put me through so much within a year now he expect me to come back like that!

It's not that easy, I can't do it. Thinking to myself walking out the door to the bus stop.

I need to hurry up and get home I been feeling sick to my stomach like everything in the bagel place smell weird.

GODS PLAN IS TO GIVE NOT ALWAYS LOOKING TO RECEIVE.

YOU WILL RECEIVE WHEN YOU LEAST EXPECT IT.

"How was work baby girl, says my mom you look sick in the face are you ok".

Before I knew it I dropped everything I had in my hand and ran to the toilet releasing all the food and fluids I had in my stomach.

"Baby you ok" What were you eating at that place today?

Take a hot shower and relax I will get everything else.

My mom so sweet, she will do anything to make sure I'm ok.

I don't know why I been feeling like this maybe once I take my shower I will feel better!

"I hate this feeling ma! I didn't eat anything at work everything smelled weird and funny to me but I didn't think anything about it.

Talking to my mother as I wrapped my dry towel around my body ."

Well honey I hope your not pregnant, your back side do look like it's spreading.

You don't have to show in your belly the baby can be held anywhere.

I need you to set a doctors appointment tomorrow when you have time.

Mom looking at me with her hand on her hip "your dad will be upset about this".

Maaaaaaa, pregnant!! I CANT BE!!! I'm not ready for that, I stopped speaking to Lamont now I might be pregnant by him, as a tear drop fall down my cheeks.

"Take the test first Shanel, let's not get beside ourselves with all the thoughts, call Lamont once you find out".

Another humiliated night I can't believe I'm about to go through a pregnancy, my father about to kill me.

I don't want to go back to cheating Lamont and I most definitely don't want his baby.

How will I look my dad in the eyes and tell him this, I need a career, a foundation, and my life in order.

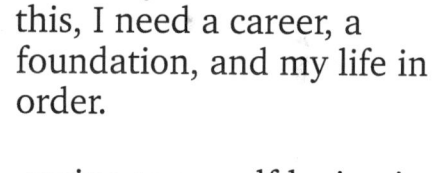

crying to myself laying in bed until I fell asleep til the next morning.

The clock reads 7:02 am I'm expecting to hear my alarm at 6:00am I jump up out my bed.
"DAMMIT IM RUNNING LATE", not today my

second day at this job I have to be at work by 8:30 to open with Terrance.

I have the biggest headache right now, after crying my night away!

I don't have time to dwell on last night let me get it together and call a cab so I'm on time to work.

"Hey baby you ok this morning" yes ma'am I'm running behind for work, are you able to take me or I can call a cab.

Mom looking at me with sadness in her eyes because she see mine without talking about how she's feeling.

Yes I will take you, she replied making our Sunday morning breakfast.

It's 7:12 Get dressed by that time the food finish you should be ready and we can leave you still have a little time.

"Thank You"! Kissing mom on her cheek leaving the kitchen to get dressed.

Ring Ring Ring!!!!! Looking over at my phone and thinking to myself (why is Lamont calling me).

When I'm ready I will talk, until then I don't have anything to say!

I'm ready mom, grabbing bacon from the stove I have the keys so I will start the car.

The conversation will start right about now, I see my mom lips moving without saying anything.

Shanel!!!! When are you going to see your doctor?

We need to know soon as possible, especially your dad you have to tell him.

"I know mother I will find out" with the cracking in my voice with scare.

8:35am exactly, I made it to work a couple minutes late but Terrance look like he's ok.

"Good morning Ms. Shanel! Look like you had a long and fun night". Smacking his lips and twisting his neck.

No Terrance I didn't, I'm just going through right now nothing to be discussed at this point.

"EXCUSE ME CAN ANYONE HELP!!! Hearing a woman's voice with anger, as she stated she's been waiting.

"GOOD MORNING Ma'am I'm sorry for your wait! How can I help you". Looking closer and noticed it was Latrina. (ugh)

Shanel!!! Hey girl you working here now (slight smile) I haven't seen or heard from you in months. Girl I see you and Lamont no longer together I be seeing him with Terri.

Yes they dating now, looking up at the menu with the rolling of her eyes.

"Terrance Terrance I need you to take this order please standing looking at Latrina with a tear in my eyes and a funny feeling to my stomach!

Running away to the bathroom to throw up. Thinking to myself (WHY) why did I have to meet him now I think I'm pregnant.

I feel so humiliated especially seeing and hearing her voice.

Girl get out here, what you doing! (Hearing Terrance voice to come back to the register). We have more customers out here.

Wiping my face and Gargling with hot water adding gum in my mouth. "On my way out," I hope Latina's gone I can't stand to hear her voice.

"You ok, you look sick don't tell me you pregnant or you have a hangover."

I'm not for sure Terrance it most definitely not a hangover.

Will it be ok if I leave so I can go to the hospital, I hate to come in late and leave early.

I'm not having the best start this morning, and I hate to leave you alone but I feel sick.

Terrance looking at me as I'm looking weak to my stomach. "Yes honey leave I will be ok your shift will be covered."

THANK YOU!!!!

A WOMAN WITH SO MUCH LOVE AND LOYALTY FOR A MAN WITH SO MUCH PRIDE, WILL NEVER UNDERSTAND UNTIL HE REALIZE AND UNDERSTAND THE TYPE OF WOMAN HE HAVE.

CHAPTER IIII

THE BREAKING POINT TO DETERMINATION

Staring at the wall with disbelief, tears falling from my eyes because I couldn't believe the news!

Doctor are you sure, you telling me I'm 5 months pregnant!

All this time I never felt a baby move, I never had any mornings sickness until a couple days ago but it's only when I smell different foods.

"Yes dear the Ultrasound shows a baby boy that looks healthy".

Your due date will be here sooner then expected, so smile you're about to be a mom!

My mind racing, my heart beating fast and my hands sweaty, thinking to myself I'm a mommy how in the world will I explain this to my father.

Putting my clothes on, as I'm listening to the doctor giving me tips for first time mothers.

"DOC!! I'M A MOM" yelling out loud to relieve my happiness, not trying to think about what my parents will say.

Thinking to myself, I'm grown!

It's my baby and I have to deal with him. 7:43 what a long day I can finally leave and go home.

"Oh my goodness now I have to call Lamont", what will he say, do he want to be a dad?

Will he be here for us? My mind racing and racing I don't know what to think!

My life is completely over at this point, why me why me putting my hand over my head not knowing what to expect.

Feeling a vibration on my leg didn't realize my phone was on silent. Looking down it's my mom!

"HEY MA", you can be on your way I'm ready. As she reply back ok!

Asking if I'm ok trying to get into details if I'm pregnant or not.

"I'm fine Ma we will talk when I see you".

This about to be a long rest of my night, Lamont about to be so extra and I really don't want to deal with him.

I guess I will call when I get home or should I tell my dad first.

Mom finally pulling up as she blinking the head light off and on so I can see her pull in.

Before I can even get in the vehicle I hear, "You did it uh, what they say".

Dang Ma, can I get in first! Can I put on my sit belt laughing but very serious.

"I'm having a boy and I'm five months pregnant".

Looking out the window with all type of thoughts going through my head.

Here she goes pressing on the brakes hard and fast, "FIVE MONTHS"!!!! Shanel did you say Five Months, where are you holding the baby let me see that ultrasound.

With that look of disbelief, my mother eyes were looking all weird like she want to strangle me.

"MA NO!!!! PLEASE DRIVE", I'm not ready to deal with this right now.

I already have to deal with Lamont and dad not you too.

Driving home in silence, she's upset and I'm furious I don't have time to deal with this but she will make time for us all to sit and talk.

Finally pulling up to the house, "Your dad about to be pissed".

You better figure out what you want to say to him before you say it, I don't want to hear his mouth because he will not stop until the baby is born.

Getting out the car rolling my eyes, she made this about her and it's my problem but I do understand.
Yes my dad will be upset with me, while he complains every second about everything. He just need to understand it's my problem not theres.

Closing the car door to walk into the house.

I see my father getting water in the kitchen but I walk directly to my room in silence, as my mother walking behind me to greet my dad with a hug and kiss.

"Betty are you ok? What's wrong with Shanel I see the sadness in her eyes everything ok", dad looking at mom as he holds her after there kiss.

Yes honey she's ok Shanel will talk to you when she's ready, but I'm tired so I'm about to get ready for bed, walking away touching his hands after she leaves his presents.

"BETTY BETTY!!!!" Y'all better tell me something why everybody in silence around her.

Listening to my dad in the kitchen waiting to see if he's about to open my bedroom door.

"SILENCE"...............

The entire house silent nobody saying a word and my dad confused. I hate doing this to him right now but I'm not ready for the leisure.

Hopefully I can go to bed and start all over in the morning. Only if this was a dream, because I don't want Lamont in it.

Dosing off to sleep hearing the squeaking of my door as if someone was entering, but it was the wind from the open window in my room.

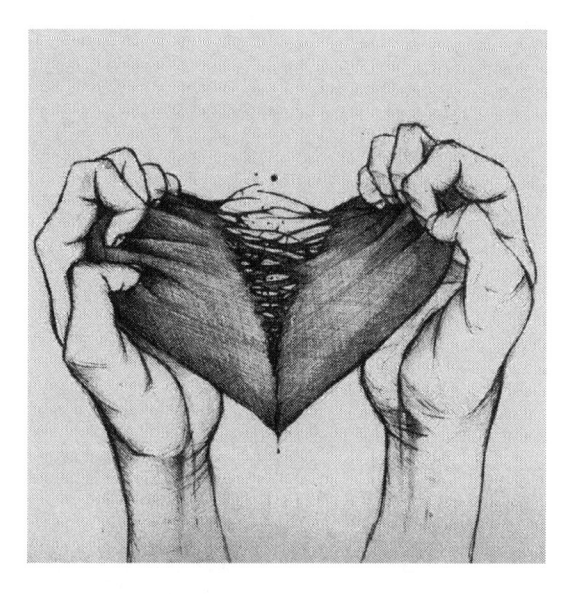

The breaking point between the couple can only be fixed when it's ready to be fixed on.

3 o'clock in the morning I started feeling weird as if I was having stomach pains, I didn't want to bother my parents so I tried to deal with it alone.

Not knowing exactly what the problem was so I started tossing and turning until I became comfortable.

I guess the baby didn't like the way I was laying across my bed.

All I can think about is that I'm pregnant and it's a boy!! I'm excited but scared and afraid.

It's funny because I guess Lamont knew I was thinking about him seeing that his name was going across my phone as it rings with the display of (Cheater).

Of course I let the phone ring and ring, I will call him later.

Shanel Call me when you wake up we need to talk.

Reading the text message that came through directly after he called.

It's been 5 to 6 months maybe longer since I last spoke with Lamont after what happened, I guess it's time to share information with him before it's too late.

10am its storming all I hear is loud thunder as I get up and my stomach feel like this baby grew over night.

I have to call in I'm not feeling up to it today, it's raining I'm not trying to catch a bus in all this mess.

Looking at my phone to see that the cheater called numerous times, I decided to call back.

"Hey Lamont" looking into the ceiling not wanting to call but I have to let him know he have a baby on the way.

I see you called me many of times what's up?

"Shanel I just want you to know I miss you and I'm sorry"! I'm sorry Baby.

Listening to Lamont beg and plead about how sorry he was, it pretty much went in and out! "Lamont I have something to say, I'm Pregnant."

Silence I can imagine Lamont face on the other side of the phone.

"PREGNANT!!!!!" Shanel I will do anything to get you back, you having my baby.

Lamont sounding exciting and enthusiastic, baby you know I'm ready to start my family. I will take it all back if I can, trust me please give me another chance.

Listening to Lamont go on and on about how much he love me, and willing to do what ever for his Jr. made me cry because it sound so cute and touching.

All I want is for my baby to have his father in his life, if I have to take it back and forget about the pass then I will.

He said he will never hurt me again and I believe him.

"OK Lamont I love you too we can raise our baby together". No more problems out of you!

These months not seeing and talking to you had me feeling down!
(Thinking to myself I hope this was worth the wait)

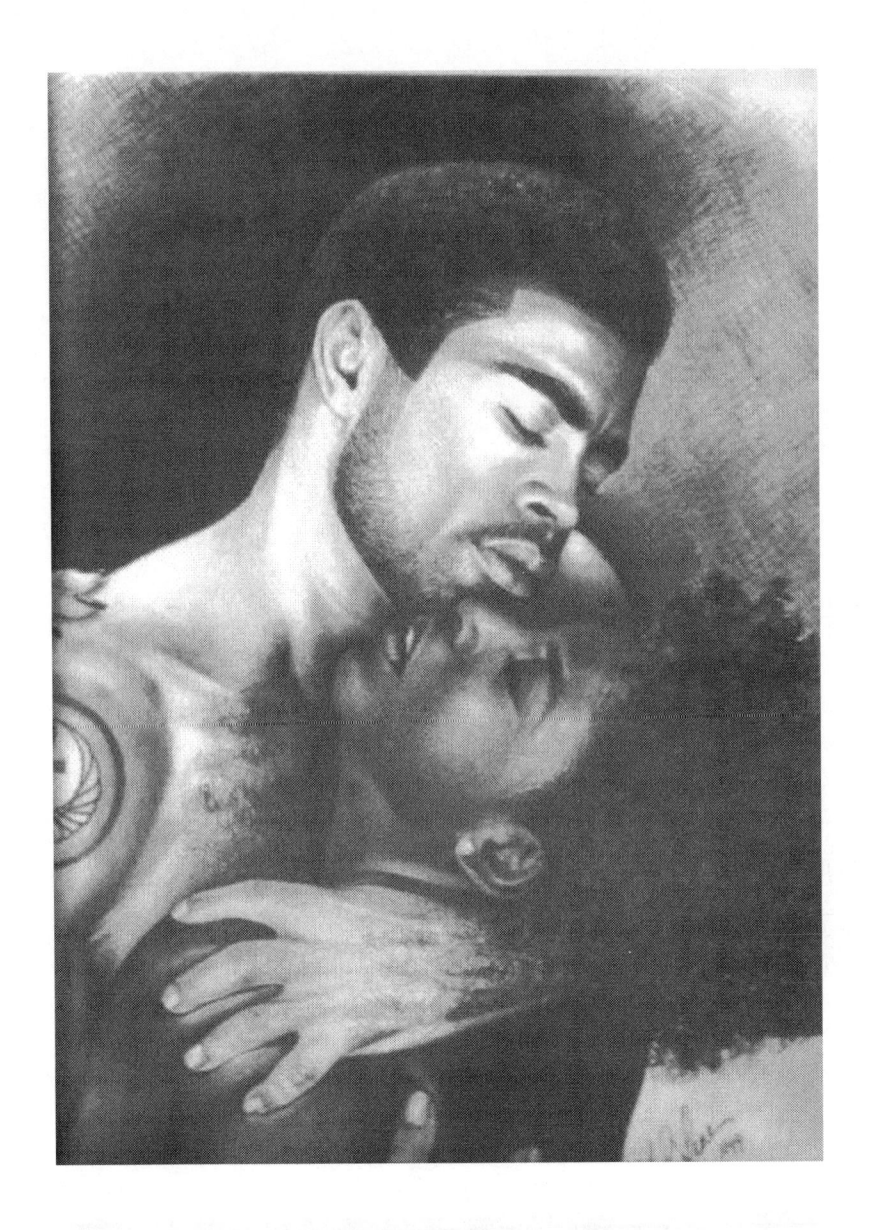

A man with flawless will either handle them alone or take his family through it because he can't handle it!

CHAPTER V

TRUST YOUR GUT WITH GOD'S WORDS

The wait is finally over, Lamont has finally decided to get himself together now that we have a baby on the way.

10am Thursday morning I here is my phone ringing off the hook, as I look down and see it's Lamont so of course this time I answered with a smile.

"Good morning baby you still sleep"? I need you to get up it's time we start looking for a apartment.

APARTMENT!!! As I blurted out without thinking (He want to move in together). "Man are you crazy! We just made up a month ago and now you want to move in together".

Thinking That's a big decision Is he really ready.

"Shanel why you always doing shit like that we have a baby on the way it's time we build our own family".

Hearing the anger from Lamont's voice like he really thought long and hard about having a family.

Lamont the way we been going and the things you put me through are you really ready for this? I trust my gut and gods words, I just don't trust him at this point.

Listening to him going on and on Blah blah blah, I'm thinking should I or wait.

Before I knew it I say "OK" all I can do now is pray.

Lamont bit his tongue after he repeated my word over! "Dam"!! Baby you ok with it?

everything will be ok trust me, I Love You Shanel.

Get dressed I will be there about 12pm as Lamont and I started to hang up our call, my mind was telling me no but my heart was saying yes I love him more then he know.

If I want to make this work I have to put my all in at this point.

Not thinking about the what if's.

Hearing three knocks on the door, whispering Shanel Shanel what you doing.

Hearing a male voice thinking to myself is that my big bro (2 Badd) as I jumped out of bed to open the door and all I feel is a tight hug with the four knuckles going across my head, as I play fight him off of me.

Man when you get home and why ma didn't tell me, watching mom standing by the bathroom room door smiling knowing how much I love and miss my brother.

He been locked up for so long Back and forth I don't know how many years he did in all. "Look at you bro all big and buff, what they been feeding you".

Looking down at my stomach as he always tried to make a joke, "nothing compared to what you been eating"! Laughing looking back at our mom as if he didn't know I was pregnant.

"Sis, I know you not pregnant! Who is this dude I need to see him talk some sense into him".

A Brother's Bond with his sisters is a bond you will never want to mess with, when the love is unconditional.

Looking at 2 Badd like he's serious, not knowing Lamont was on his way over shortly and that I'm moving out with him. "Well bro since you and mom here I can tell y'all that I'm moving out and my boyfriend Lamont on his way if you want to meet him."

Mom looking at 2 Bad, he's looking at me and I'm looking at the both of them.

"WHAT"!!!!

Girl do you know what you about to get yourself into, when your father get back you already know his head about to spin, as my mother sounding disappointed about my decision.

I keep thinking to myself it's not right but I'm having a baby and I want him to know his father, I grew up with mine why break the chain now replying back with eager.

Watching my brother shake his head back and forth, buzz buzzz hearing the door bell ring as I run into my room look on phone and see Lamont called back to back, and I'm not ready!

My brother here now I have to introduce them putting my hand on head in a complete rush.

"Let me answer the door so I can meet this dude Lamont, that's his name right"?

2 Badd sounding so aggressive WHO IS IT!! Hearing the name of Lamont as he opens the door and see this tall guy 6'1 with a wave nouveau.

First thing come to my brother mind is Lamont one of those east side boys. Looking him up and down "WHATS UP AND YOU ARE? MATTER OF FACT WHAT SET YOU ON.

Lamont giving this look I never seen before like who is this man talking to. Now my brother want to get into his street and jail talk.

Before you two start Lamont this my oldest brother
   2 Badd as he continues to ask questions, we have to leave Bro will see you soon snatching Lamont out the door to the car.

"Dam Shanel so that's how you let niggas talk to me", I didn't see you say a word.

Excuse me, that nigga is my brother so don't call him that and for your information I had more then enough to say that's why we left, LAMONT. Don't

start with me I was having some what of a good day!

Who you talking too, as Lamont had this angry look in his eyes like he wanted to hit me. Do tell me what your day is like I said you didn't do nothing, got dude in my face like I'm a kid or something.

He don't know me but he can the next time he in face like that. I'm sitting in my seat thinking, I really don't want this relationship.

"Yea ok Lamont I'm ready to go back home", I don't think I'm ready for this right now. Before I knew it he had the meanest look in his eyes I'm looking like what is he thinking right now.

"Bitch you got me fucked up if you think I'm about to keep coming to your parents house to see my son". Grown up and be a woman so we can raise my baby.

Once I heard Lamont disrespect me like he did, I felt hurt knowing it was that easy to say that to me with no hesitation or remorse. "REALLY LAMONT!!!

So I'm a bitch you mad and upset taking your issue out on me why? I did nothing to be disrespected like this, NOW TAKE ME HOME.

"I'm sorry baby your brother rubbed me the wrong way, with his approach". No type of way to talk to a man you don't know.

I understand where Lamont coming from but name calling is not how you suppose to solve the problem taking it out on me. If he's doing this what else should I be aware of?

"Lamont I never had a man talk to me like that before and I don't want to start ".

Looking with anger in my eyes as we pull up to my parents house, I will figure this out later when he have a new attitude.

My gut is really telling me not to move in with this man but I don't know what to do. I don't want

to leave my parents, and I don't want to live in the house with a man I don't completely trust yet.

Pulling up to my parents house Lamont look sad in the face as he always do when he know he's wrong. "I'm sorry Baby, I been so defensive lately I just want everything to right for my little man that's all".

You out of all people should understand where I'm coming from. Once again as he always do very charming! And he gets me every time as I fall for it.

"I understand Lamont I want our baby to be ok. We can try again tomorrow, I will look in the newspaper my dad have and mark some places".

Giving Lamont a hug and kiss goodbye, as I opened the door to get out the car, he's watching me making sure I get inside safely before pulling off.

A black man will be the king but the voice and tone he uses will not allow him to, the tongue he received from his father can make him less of the man he supposed to be if not used correctly towards the Queen of his child.

"So that's your baby daddy little sis, what you see in him"?

Listening to my brother before I can make it up stairs to my room.

2 Badd don't start with me, you out of all people have the audacity to ask me questions when you never around to see what I go through.

"You my oldest brother you come and go in and out of jail when we need you the most at home"!

It's time he know exactly how I feel, my brother never was around when needed but when he do come we know and others did too it's like the whole scenery change.

My brother is born hustler got into a gang organization about 14 yrs old hanging around the streets of Illinois.

He have no filter all he knew was money you will either live by it or die by it. Years and years being incarcerated he gain more knowledge that others didn't understand but he knew the game of a true OG Hustler.

I guess that's why I love him some much, all the times he was locked up he made sure I knew the streets just as well as he did.

"Sis now you know I'm not starting with you I just need to know what dude about and what he on".

I know how these scrubs get down I will hurt a nigga over my baby sister. Laughing and grabbing me with a gentle brotherly hug.
Thanks bro but we good, you will know be before anybody as I walked into my room to lay across my bed.

I hope I know what I'm doing, having a baby and about to move in with his father, throwing the pillow over my face to release a slight scream so I can't be heard.

"Sis you good"? "YESSS"! THANK YOU!! Replying back.

Now that's over time I look into the newspaper rental section to find us a apartment.

7pm the house quiet bro gone, mom gone and pops still out of town. He's about to ring my neck when he gets back home, I'm pregnant out of wedlock and about to move in with a man I don't trust.

I'm thinking about writing him a letter and leave it as that, I can't stand to see his face knowing his nineteen year old baby girl about to have a baby.

Daddy's girl will always be a fathers baby, it don't matter how old you are your still his little girl.

It's been a long night I just want some breakfast and go to work, these last couple of days been crazy and I just want a clear mind putting everything behind me. Getting out my bed to start a new week without all the drama with my Lamont.

Did everybody make it home safely it's so quiet in this house, walking out my room and smell bacon thinking (Yes she's making breakfast) look again and it's 2 BaDD cooking for himself.

"What's up sis you good, you hungry"? I made enough as he's making a plate. I hope you slept good not thinking about ole boy, because right now I don't like him.

Thanks bro I'm good knowing dam well he can't cook, I already know how you feel about Lamont and that's ok he's my sons father so all that matters is that he's here for us.

"No problem Sis I will stay out of your business but he better do right by you and my nephew, I don't want to put hands on this man" as we both laughed out loud but very serious.

I LOVE YOU SIS!!! 2 BaDD loving smile that makes us all melt knowing he's my charming brother.

"Well I'm about to get ready for work I been off about a couple of days I hope I still work there, shrugging my shoulders as if I didn't care.

"LOVE YOU MORE BIG BRO", walking back to my room to get dressed and ready to be out the house by 10:30am. Lamont called sounding so nice, that he will be picking me up soon. I guess we will try this again without the arguing and demanding.

Time is ticking and Lamont still have not made it here yet knowing I have to be at work by 10:45am.

Unbelievable I hope nothing happened because if it didn't it will, it's already 10:40 oh my goodness as I'm listening to my phone ring about three times and see Lamont's name going across my screen. Thinking to myself, "I know he's not calling me and not here.

Answering "WHAT", why you not here yet Lamont, you know I have to be at work by 10:45.

"Baby that's my fault I had to make a stop and didn't see the time, on my way now, call them let them know you running late".

As I listen to Lamont and his lies, staring at my wall thinking to myself why! I hung up before he was able to say anything else.

"Shanel you ok Lil sis"? Seeing my brother walk into my room as he see me in a zone. I was checking on you I over heard dude on the phone, let's go I will drop you off to work I never want you to wait on a man for nothing.

Once again I was so disappointed in Lamont and still made the decision to move in knowing my brother and mother didn't agree, and I still have not told my dad.

Quarter to one and Lamont calling my phone stating he's at my door, I dam near cussed him out.

"Two hours later and you finally made it my house goodbye".

I'm so sick of him all he do is drink and smoke, barely working a nine to five job.

I always think what am I getting myself into, I don't like this man but I'm having his baby.

This decision is based on my child not my love and I hate the fact of me going through it.

"Shanel we need you in the office please", as management call me off the work floor.

We have been watching your performance since you been on probation and we have noticed too many absences, call ins and late performance from you.

We absolutely love your work but we're sorry we have to let you go today, you can clock out and remove your things immediately.

My face expression tell it all, I can't believe this! They firing me, they could of told me this while I was home over the phone.

Instead they had me wasting gas money and my time dealing with Lamont lying ass. Walking away from looking at Terrance all he was able to say was "Sorry Girl" with his twist of the neck. I'm so tired of the back and forth working job after job, listening to lies and dealing with uncomforted in my life.

Father God please help me find who I am as a woman and your child. I can't do this without you, please help me.

Gathering all my things to leave I didn't want to call anyone so I caught the bus back home to see that my dad made it back in town. Oh my goodness I'm glad the baby still not showing as much, my dad just think I'm fat anyways so he can't tell.

Hey daddy I see you made back I thought you were coming in tomorrow morning? Look like you had a lot of fun I wish I was there.

"Hi daughter the reunion was great had a chance to see all my high school buddies". You would of enjoyed yourself in south baby girl, what's wrong Shanel I see your face looking chunky what your momma been cooking while I been gone.

Laughing to myself only if you knew dad. I'm good father, I was just fired from the bagel place I'm just sick of working for people.

"Figure it out baby, figure it out" as dad walk away with the kiss to my forehead of love.

I will figure it out but first I need to tell you about this baby, as I go into the house to my room.

God plan is always the best, sometimes the process is painful and hard but don't forget that when God's silent. He's doing something good for you.

CHAPTER VI

FAMILY FIRST TIL DEATH DO US PART

Lamont and I finally rented a home together, I'm sitting outside on the porch reminiscing feeling the breeze drinking my sparkle water thinking about the good and bad times, when I first met Lamont, how he went from good to disrespectful, the cheating, how I didn't trust him anymore, how I was scared to tell my dad about my pregnancy, the arguments, my brother watching him without knowing, my other two children plus the one I'm pregnant with now.

This brought me to realize I been through a lot with this man and now he's talking about marriage.

It's the summer 2002 I'm almost due with my third child.

This baby came out of nowhere the unexpected one that I know will be my golden child, I didn't want anymore by this man but he's here.

The more we argue the more he became insecure and abusive to the point I wanted to hurt myself but couldn't because of our children.

I just want out of this relationship, my way was to get out the wrong way by hurting myself.

The hurt and pain you receive from the ones that suppose to love and care for you, will take you out due to there insecurities, hatred and envy.

Once we started our family, Lamont true colors came out. He never cared how he spoke to me or who was in front of us to hear or see it.

All I knew was, he wanted to be the man and in his mind the woman had to be obedient even when he didn't deserve the king treatment.

Doing the times we argued and fought I always thought I was doing him wrong and that I was the reason to trigger him off I want to correct these things, but he never changed.

Lamont showed me what I didn't want in this relationship. But he ask me for my hand in marriage.

something I didn't understand until I thought long and hard, it wasn't love.

It was having a wife with his children so he didn't have to pay child support.

He never loved me the way I should be loved, a man that truly care for his mate and children will never allow them to be unhappy.

I feel like a scarred mother with insecurities that's scared to leave the father of my children that drinks daily and get high off marijuana, working a job that barley pay the bills.

I can never leave Lamont he always tell me he's the only man that want me because nobody want a woman with all these children.

It was like he was trying to break me and make my life miserable without me knowing.

Baby after baby after baby, I'm learning now the more I see the things he do to me tells me what I don't need in relationship again.

Sometimes we have to bump our heads but learn how not to do it over and over again.

I guess I have to blame myself, I had many of signs that I ignored because I thought he was a great man and will be a awesome father to his children.

It's only right to have my children's father in there life no matter what the consequences are, I have to love a man that really don't love me.

"Til death do us apart"

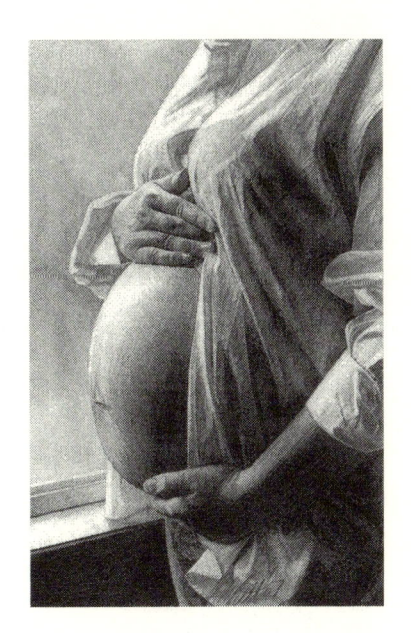

Watching Lamont walk into our home is a complete drainage, I hate to see him come into to the door at times and I'm really sick of complaining to family members about his insecure, and hateful ways.

They all tell me to pray and trust the word, only if they knew "I DO IT ALL"!

Grabbing my stomach in pain as I'm getting out my chair walking into the house to tell Lamont, "I THINK THE BABY IS COMING"!

Grabbing all my things, Shanel are you sure, as Lamont panicking racing back and forth not knowing exactly what to do.

"Yes I'm sure it hurts", rushing to the car to head to the hospital.

Thinking to myself no more babies, I can't do this this anymore. Thank god our other two children with there grandparents which made this easy for us to have this last kid with them running around.

"LAMONT HURRY UP" screaming to the top of my lungs, squeezing Lamont hand breathing in and out. The contractions are coming back to back as I'm crying trying not to push.

We finally made it to the hospital as I was getting out the car to be wheeled in my water broke, it was time to push.

So of course I started screaming, the nurse rushed me to the delivery room where I continued to push, scream and cry calling Lamonts name.

"Shanel I'm here baby keep pushing" the baby almost out, come on you can do it wiping the sweat from my forehead.

Lamont it hurts, giving that one last push hearing the nurses in the background "GREAT JOB SHANEL, YOU DID IT"!

My handsome baby boy finally made it to the outside world, weighing 6pds 9oz.

As I'm holding him and Lamont looking down at our new bundle of joy giving us a smile of happiness. "I'm proud of you Shanel you did it"! Kissing me on the lips and our baby on the forehead.

Laying in the hospital bed watching my little boy suck on his fingers brought me happiness again, looking at him nothing mattered to me beside my three children and a plan.

A mother's bundle of joy will always be the greatest blessing ever in her life, to know her body is able to hold something so cute and precious.

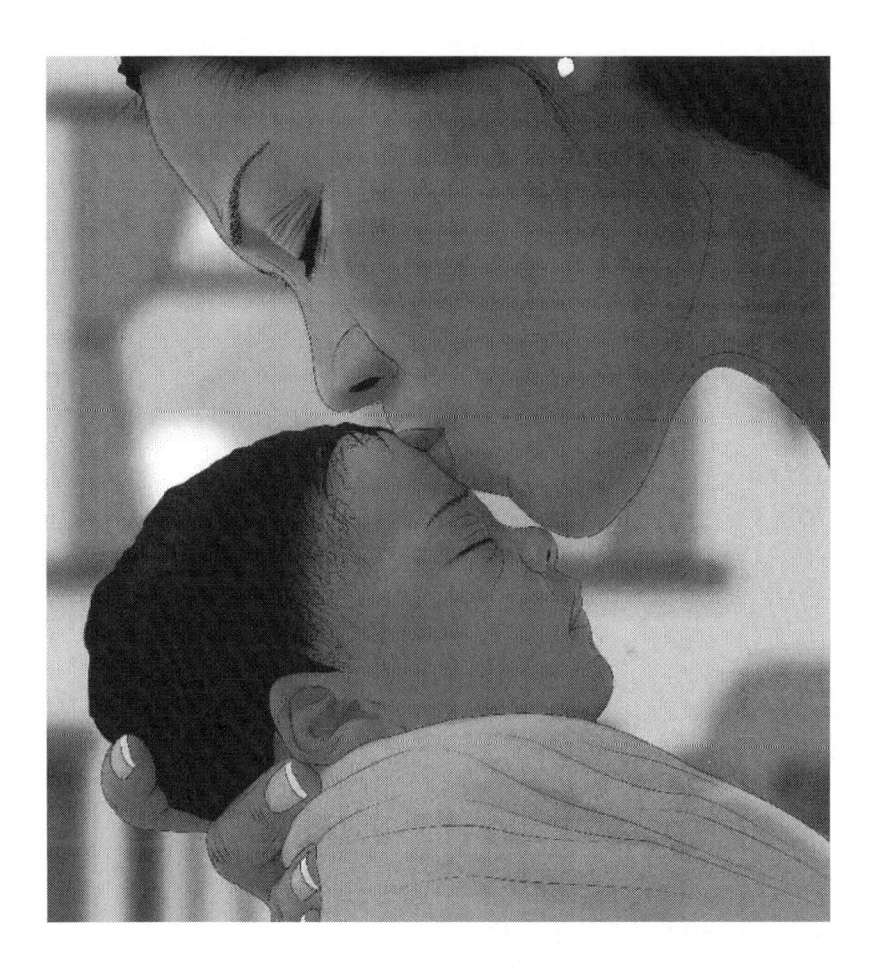

Looking over to the side of me seeing Lamont sleeping on the chair made tears form into my eyes as I'm praying and wishing for happiness with him.

I know we have to go through ups and downs in our relationship, but do it have to hurt as much as it do.

Lamont can really be a great man if he stop and realize how great of woman I am to him, and stop trying to bully me and just be the man a woman needs.

"Where you going"?

Hearing Lamont as he's ready to leave the hospital at 3:45am, like where are you going this early. Nothings open and the children with my parents.

"Dam Shanel I'm uncomfortable and hungry, so I'm going home". I will be back later why you catching a attitude for nothing, you comfortable and the baby but I'm on that hard ass chair catching a crook in my neck.

Whatever Lamont see you later as he come to peck me on the lips like I just irritated him.

I just feel like he could of asked for a blanket and pillow to make himself comfortable if he really wanted to be here.

As Lamont walking out my nurse walking in.

"Hello Ms. Houston, My name is Nurse Karen I just want to make sure your comfortable and everything's ok".

I know it can get really cold in your hospital room which I will turn the air down a little for you, but if needed please hit the button and I will be right in.

Thank you Nurse Karen, I appreciate you "can you please bring some ice".

As we continued our conversation back and forth, explaining how my sons father left because he was uncomfortable, which she said the same thing as I did.

He could of made himself comfortable if he really wanted to.

A man with many agendas will never make you his priority because he's too busy trying to Juggle them all at once.

If loving you is wrong, I don't wanna be right by Luther Ingram came on the radio as I was laying in my hospital bed breast feeding my baby.

I said I don't want to love, if I'm not getting the same love back.

It's very complicated but I will break through it. Lamont finally decided to come back to the hospital walking into my room with my other two children, ITS A BOY balloons and dozens of red roses.

"Thank you baby for being a great mother to our children I LOVE YOU SHANEL".

Not knowing my morning will start like this but he melts my heart every time when he's nice and polite.

Thank you Lamont I LOVE YOU TOO! Looking down at my oldest son and baby girl as they smile ear to ear seeing that they have a new baby brother.

"Mommy I want to hold him", says my oldest son as he reaches up to grab for his brother.

Have a seat in the chair son your to small, as his dad show him how to hold the baby gently putting baby three into his brother arms.

They so cute, glancing over seeing baby girl with her thumb in her mouth looking upset because she's not the baby anymore.

That was not the look I was going for, "La'Mira what wrong? Why are you looking sad"?

Batting her big beautiful eyes saying nothing standing there with her thumb in mouth rubbing on her belly button.

We all looked at her and her dad grabbed her giving her the biggest hug ever.

Knock on the door "Good morning it's me" seeing more balloons and and flowers held by my dad as him and my mother walk into the door.

"HI MOMMY AND DAD" Thank you for the gifts.

It was so much joy seeing them walk in, as we all talked and enjoyed the moment of our new bundle, watching the children bond with there baby brother.

It was a great day the nurse came in did my vitals stating I was able to go home tomorrow morning, showing the baby and I was healthy and great.

5pm everybody left my hospital room I feel so nice and cozy, it quiet and my baby sleeping across my chest as I'm watching television dosing off to sleep.

Thinking will anything change with Lamont ways and attitude, this is our third child will he make a difference within him for the better of our family or remain the same.

Dosing completely off to sleep, til the next morning.

Time going so fast I have to get up, bathe myself and wipe my baby down so we can leave.

Lamont will be here soon I hope he have the right car seat, the nurses here will not allow us to leave unless we have the proper vehicle car seat, I love there safety procedures.

A woman with so much power and obedience can have whom ever and what ever she wants.

But in order for her to do so, she need to know what she want in order to receive it.

We finally pull up to our house, home sweet home.

I just want to lay in my own bed and eat my own food, returning all my congratulation calls and text messages.

Walking into the house Lamont have it so clean and smelling nice.

Our bedroom smells so good he have my favorite candles burning (apple spice).

Once again he knows how to melt my heart when he want too, it's the other side of him I don't like.

"How you feeling baby"? I just wanted you to come home and rest, as you see I cleaned everything up, I will run your bubble bath later giving you more time to relax. Kissing me on my lips, my neck and grabbing my hand giving me the gentleman kiss.

"Thank you Lamont" smiling with happiness praying that it last. m

THE family THAT PRAYS TOGETHER STAYS together

As time goes on our children gets older Lamont try and try to be a better man, showing us that he care and love us then he pops the question.

"Shanel Houston Will You Marry Me".

I was startled didn't know exactly what to say because this will be my second proposal to officially say yes this time.

"YES LAMONT YES I WILL MARRY YOU" giving him the biggest hug and kiss with no regrets or bad thought crossing my mind.

I'm about to be a wife! Then I thought to myself where's my dam ring?

Lamont where's my ring? You asked for my hand in Marriage but no ring.

Boy are you playing with me I don't have time for jokes.

Looking at him with a straight attitude, "Lady Ain't nobody playing with you, I will have your ring stop getting mad at me taking it off and throwing it, you will have one".

As Lamont laugh at me like I was being funny.

I don't want to keep going back and forth what we been through taking all the bad habits into our marriage.

let's make it better this time when I get my ring better then before.

I said I DO!

Which means I'm getting married so I don't want to get upset and remove my ring.

I will have your last name it's time we do better for our children Lamont.

I'm not afraid anymore because you showed me that you can be a better man now, you been here to help more, love us and your interacting more with us like a family.

Breaking down to Lamont hopefully he hears me and not allowing it to go in his ear and out. I really do love this man I just want him to do right.

So let me get ready to start getting my wedding together I'm so excited I always wanted to be a bridezilla.

Let's get started, as I continued to call my Besties Qualla, Sonika and Shenile to meet me at home, talking to them brought us nothing more then joy and excitement.

They wanted to talk about my bachelorette party I was talking about wedding colors.

"Bye, see y'all shorty so hurry up and get over here"!

Door bell rings ten minutes after each other until they all were at my house at the same time.

"Where's the drinks and smoke", as Sonika goes into the kitchen looking around. I knew I should of stopped before I came here.

"Best friend are you really ready for this? You already know how Lamont can be but I guess it's for better or worst til death do you apart".

Listening to my crazy BFF Sonika with no filter, say what she feel and what she feel she will say it.

Of course she's ready, she would of never said yes if she wasn't. Right Friend tell her you ready,

listening to Shenile reply back to Sonika.

Shenile's more of our humble spiritual friend that keep us all together.
Listening to them go back and forth was hilarious, we sat and talked as Qualla our friend that do it all, decide to go to the store and get drinks.

Our night was great we laughed it away, making sure I was comfortable and ready to be a bride to the father of my children.

April 29th as agreed will be our wedding date my fathers birthday and also the day we buried my favorite cousin.

Time goes so fast I will be married before I know it, and we have a lot to do even though my parents will pay for everything, I just want it all to fall into place.

The joy of two people that comes together to reunite there love for one another, will be the greatest and best love that will last for eternity.

CHAPTER VII

SPIRITUAL HEALING

We did!! We finally jumped the broom I am officially Mrs. Cobblestone.

Our wedding was beautiful the reception held 250 people we danced and partied all night, my parents,

Matron of honor and maid of honor did a awesome job with everything. The balloon bouquets, the table designs, food, balloon drop and my six tier Strawberry cream cake, so delicious.

Glory to God thanking him for allowing that day to happen until the end. My husband was drunk he left me I couldn't find him and when I did we argued curse words were thrown back and forth it was unbearable.

Later that night we were dropped off by a friend as he helped Lamont in the house, telling me how sorry he was because of what my husband put me through and how he embarrassed me in front of people.

It was like a full moon once the clock hit 12' my husband turned into the big bad werewolf, it was a complete nightmare.

We got home my husband passed out drunk and sleep, I was very upset no honeymoon or a happy ending.

I felt like a angry black woman ready to leave and enjoy my night without him but instead because I'm a wife.

I took off our wedding attire, relaxed and helped no into bed as I climbed in kissing his forehead, please try try and rapping his arms around me.

"Baby I'm sorry", hearing Lamont slurring his words. You hear me talking to you, I'm sorry I messed up Shanel!

Lamont know I'm upset but I can't just get up and leave anymore I have a husband now and it's about to be a long road with Gods help and direction to get me through it all.

I will get up in a second to make coffee for us this way hopefully he can sober up and let me enjoy my little honeymoon.

"Lamont I hear you, I'm about to get you something so you can feel better".

Matter a fact get up! You owe me a honeymoon your drunk ass embarrassed me last night and your friend had to drop us off.

"I don't understand you at times" you wasn't at a friends house on there couch kicking it we got married and you couldn't hold your liquor, it's like you always trying to sabotage my happiness with you to see how far I will allow you to go.

I will not go through what I been through 10 yrs ago or I will take our children and walk away, never looking back.

"SHANEL SHUT THE FUCK UP".

Lamont have to be drunk talking to me like that because he really showing out, guess what I will shut up right after I shower and leave him in that bed.

I will go to meet up with my friends, I don't have time for him today. Lamont was more then enough last night, I don't like that man.

Looking at him right now make me want to knock him up side the head with something, he's unbelievable and he's ok with talking to me the way he do.

As Lamont continue to to lay in bed sleeping I decided to shower, get dressed and leave.

Going to my child hood friend Shenile's house will help me out a lot more then then me trying to kill him.

(Ding dong) standing outside on this warm sunny day looking cute outside ringing Shenile door bell, answer the door girl I'm tired of waiting out here you knew I was coming over.

I thought sharing what happened at my wedding with my best friend will mean so much especially with her being so spiritual.

She know exactly what to say keeping me in good spirit with positive energy.

Good friends are hard to find especially the genuine ones that truly love you like a sister and care about your well being.

That will be there through thick and thin no matter what the circumstances are, you have a friend like that keep them.

Soon as I started to talk to Shenile more and more the door bell started to ring and she was looking suspicious. "Shenile who did you invite over"? Doing something you have no business doing.

"Well Sonika and Qualla, it's best that we are all here to hear your cry's as we all come together in prayer asking that your covered in the blood of Jesus Christ".

With out him there's no us as we pray for greatness over our life and your her new husband.

Father Protect, Guide and strengthen us giving healing and success almighty high, keeping us out of harms way as you cover and protect our children from evilness.

   Shenile spoke in tongue over us all as she always do with her crystals and burning sage as we all sip wine keeping faith in my marriage. One thing for sure my friends never say the words **I told you so.**

   It's late and Lamont haven't called me once typical and heart breaking.

   I tell myself over and over it will get better but nothing changed besides my last name.

   Only time will tell, weeks going by the children seeing us arguing, cursing, yelling and fighting same old shit different days.

   November 2006 I can't take it anymore, we tried many of times to accommodate each other needs and wants but nothing work when you go back to the old you.

   So it's time to act accordingly especially when I'm a great mother and awesome wife.

   I work my ass off so my children will have it all and not ask for it, everything I do is for them.

   Down the road I pray they see my plan was for better not to remain cooped in a small 2 bedroom home with three children.

I want better and for my children to know their worth not wish for it, seeing what others have and they don't.

Lamont never liked the way I raised our children he always complained they were too spoiled and they don't know how to value a dollar, well show them.

Never complain about what you don't have especially when you can get it. Know who you are as a man or woman, know your value on how much you can take in and what your able to give out.

Know Your Worth

Three days after Thanksgiving I prayed on it, read my bible, spoke to God, ask for forgiveness and cried and with it all being said I'm still directed back to divorcing my husband.

When a woman fed up she is fed up, especially if I tried for eleven years and we haven't accomplished anything just wasted years of alcohol, sex, trauma, cheating, marijuana, pain, hurt, distraction, lies, abuse, hate and tears.

Time is up!

Lamont made it clear it really don't want a family he just want another mother, somebody to take care of him while he do whatever, whenever, and however.

It's time I go back to church to receive my healing, I asked my husband so many times to go with me and he stated he's not ready to be in a church.

That's when I should of told him that he's not ready to be my husband.

CHAPTER VIII

POWER

"I did it! I'm finally a free woman".

Months and months trying to contact Lamont to sign all the documents for this divorce.

Lamont made me search for him until I made that last call to come to the court because I was tired of playing his games, keeping me from having my own personal life with my children without all the drama and disrespect.

"Shanel is this what you want? You know once I sign there's no coming back". I love you and this how you do me.

Knowing everything he was saying was a complete front for his friends and family to make it look as if I did him wrong and he was the innocent one.

"Boy sign the paper so we can go, there's nothing else to be said or explained, I'm ready to go I have plans set to live a great life and your wasting my time holding me back".

After we all signed the the divorce papers I was able to keep my last name this way I still have the name I worked hard for, to show my children I didn't break.

I wanted to show them that I'm a Strong mother and I'm willing to keep the same name as theres.

Looking at my cellphone seeing so many cheerful messages hip hop hooray, yes hunty, you did that and girl let's celebrate.

I never knew how it felt to have a load of bull crap removed out my life until now, it feel so good.

As we all walked out the court room I have a peace of mind giving praise to our Heavenly Father.

Without you I would of never removed myself out of this abusive relationship.

I have my power back, and there's nothing to stop me or hold me back from being a better me.

Never loose who you are as a human being

because you want to impress others.

Have your own mindset nobody knows you better then you.

Power in the **Bible** has deeper **meaning** than we can imagine.

It's also frequently used in the book as description of strength of mind, moral qualities of a person, **power** of his/her faith. It means that this person or God has some inner strength that does not depend on outward things.

In Loving Memories Arthur L. Hudson (Too Badd)

The power will always be within you, never become to comfortable and let go.

Made in the USA
Columbia, SC
09 May 2021